Jacques
griffe.
1 mistigri

CATS, CATS, CATS

Dear Sadie,

Hope you're not planning a trip to Memphis anytime soon. No offense.

Your cousin,

Pearl

CATS, CATS, CATS

sam

andy Warhol

ANDY WARHOL

A BULFINCH PRESS BOOK

LITTLE, BROWN AND COMPANY BOSTON NEW YORK LONDON

First Edition
Seventh Printing, 2000
Quotations from Andy Warhol compiled by R. Seth Bright
Designed by John Kane

Library of Congress Cataloging-in-Publication Data

Warhol, Andy, 1928–1987
    Cats, cats, cats / Andy Warhol. —1st ed.
      p. cm.
    "A Bulfinch Press Book"
    ISBN 0-8212-2130-2
    1. Warhol, Andy, 1928–1987—Catalogs. 2. Warhol, Andy, 1928–1987-
Quotations. 3. Cats in art. I. Title.
NC139.W37A4 1994
741.973—dc20   94-13440

Bulfinch Press is an imprint and trademark of
Little, Brown and Company (Inc.)

PRINTED IN SINGAPORE

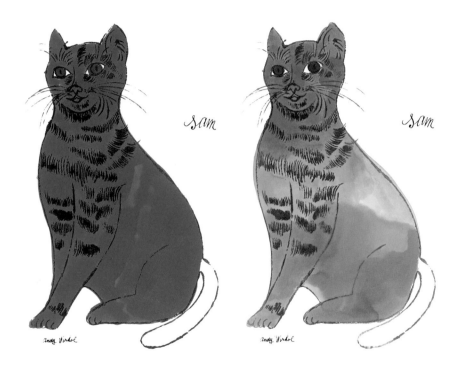

Sam

Sam

I never *met an* animal *I didn't* like.

It's **all** in your attitude.

People,

I think,

are the only things that know how to take up

more space

than the space they're actually in.

I'd prefer

to remain a mystery.

I love animals.

I once had twenty-six cats.

25 Cats name Sam
and
one Blue
Pussy

By
andy Warhol

Sam

To have a
really good time,

you don't have to actually
look good,

you just have to *think* that you do.

When you want to be **like** something,

it means you really

love it.

andy Warhol

The important thing is to infuse everything with as much drama as you can.

I always notice flowers.

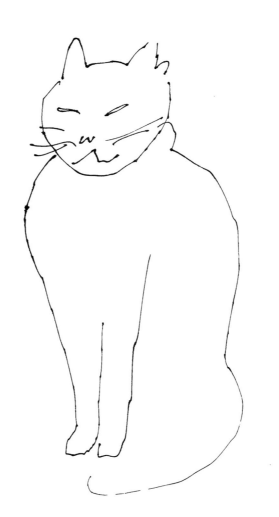

I wish she'd just let me sleep.

Being smart could make you depressed, certainly, if you weren't smart about what you were smart about.

It's viewpoint that's important.

Somehow, the way life works, people usually wind up either in crowded subways and elevators, or in

big rooms

all by themselves.

Everybody should have a **big room** they can go to

and everybody should also ride the crowded subways.

It's **not**
what you are that counts,

it's **what they *think***
you are.

sam

Andy Warhol

Being **clean** is so important.

The less something has to say,

the **more** perfect it is.

Andy Warhol

I've always just tried to do things that make people laugh.

You have to be willing to get

happy about nothing.

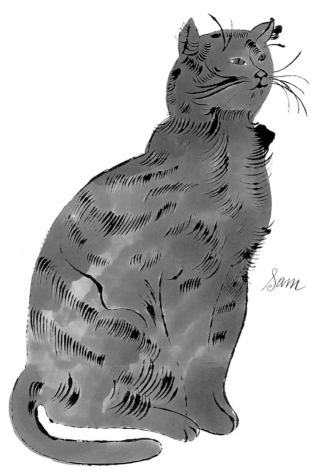

Sam

Andy Warhol

I don't think it matters

how I'm appreciated,

levels

on

many

or just one.

Since I found out he has a secret life and sleeps out a lot,

I don't feel responsible for him.

25
cats
named

SAM

Sam

Muscles are great.

Everybody should have at least

one they can
show off.

Because

if you can't mingle at all,

that's when you really get

nutty.

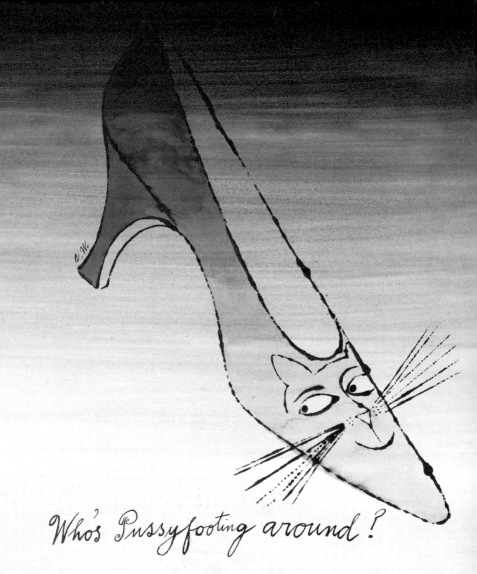

Who's Pussyfooting around?

I love the sound of people's voices.

I love people.

What

makes a person spend time
being sad

when they could be

happy?

SAM

I still think it's nice to care about people.

As I always say,

one's   company,

two's   a crowd,

three's a party.

meow

Jacque griffe
mistyri

meow

She was **mysterious** and **European,**

a real
moon goddess
type.

andy Warhol

People were always getting

dressed up

for a party.

By living in one room you eliminate a lot of worries. But the basic worries, unfortunately, remain:

Are the lights on or off?

Is the water off?

Are the cigarettes out?

Is the back door closed?

Is the elevator working?

Is there anyone in the lobby?

Who's that sitting in my lap?

Sam

Pets make a family loyal, that's always will do just about anything to make you happy, never criticize, love you till the end of the earth, and never expect much in return.

Pets are really the answer.

All quotes are by Andy Warhol
and were first published as follows:

Pages 18, 26, 29, 33, 50, 60:
Andy Warhol. *The Philosophy of Andy Warhol (from A to B and Back Again)*. New York: Harcourt Brace Jovanovich, 1975.

Pages 7, 46, 63, 64:
Andy Warhol. *America*. New York: Harper & Row, 1985.

Page 30:
Andy Warhol and Pat Hackett. *POPism: The Warhol 60s*. New York: Harcourt Brace Jovanovich, 1980.

Pages 8, 17, 21, 22, 38:
Andy Warhol and Pat Hackett. *Andy Warhol's Party Book*. New York: Crown Publishers, 1988.

Pages 25, 42:
Pat Hackett, Editor. *The Andy Warhol Diaries*. New York: Warner Books, 1989.

Pages 11, 12-13, 14, 34, 37, 40, 45, 49, 53, 54, 56, 59:
Mike Wrenn. *Andy Warhol: In His Own Words*. London: Omnibus Press, 1991.

Captions by page number

Cover

Untitled (Cat), c. 1956
Ink, Dr. Martin's Aniline Dye
on Strathmore paper
22 7/8" x 14"

Endpaper

*Sketch for Bonwit Teller Window
Display*, c. 1955
Ink on manila paper
14" x 16 3/4"

3   *Cat ("25 Cats Named Sam…")*,
    c. 1954
    Hand-colored offset print
    9 1/8" x 6"

5   *Cat*, c. 1954
    Ink on paper
    16 3/4" x 13 7/8"

6A *Cat ("25 Cats Named Sam…")*,
    c. 1954
    Hand-colored offset print
    9 1/8" x 6"

6B *Cat ("25 Cats Named Sam…")*,
    c. 1954
    Hand-colored offset print
    9 1/8" x 6"

9   *Cat*, c. 1957
    Black ballpoint on white paper
    13 7/8" x 18"

10 *Two Kittens ("25 Cats Named
    Sam…")*, c. 1954
    Hand-colored offset print
    9 1/8" x 6"

12-13
    Cat, c. 1957
    Ink on paper
    11 1/4" x 17 7/8"

15 *Cover ("25 Cats Named Sam…")*,
    c. 1954
    Hand-colored offset print
    9 1/8" x 6"

16 *Cat*, c. 1955
    Ink, Dr. Martin's Aniline Dye,
    and printed material on paper
    18 1/8" x 13 1/4"

19   *Two Reclining Kittens*, c. 1954
Ink on paper
17" x 14"

20   *Cat ("25 Cats Named Sam…")*,
c. 1954
Hand-colored offset print
9 1/8" x 6"

23   Same as cover

24   *Cat*, c. 1954
Ink on paper
11 3/4" x 8 7/8"

27   *Seated Cat*, c. 1956
Gold leaf and ink on
Strathmore paper
22 7/8" x 14 1/4"

28   *Untitled (Cat in Front of Church)*,
c. 1959
Ink, graphite, Dr. Martin's
Aniline Dye on Strathmore
paper
23" x 14 5/8"

31   *Untitled (Cat)*, c. 1956
Ink, Dr. Martin's Aniline Dye
on Strathmore paper
23" x 14 5/8"

32   *Seated Cat (Sam)*, c. 1954
Ink on Strathmore paper
23" x 14 5/8"

35   *Cat*, c. 1957
Ink on paper
14" x 17 7/8"

36   *Cat*, c. 1956
Ink, Dr. Martin's Aniline Dye,
and ballpoint on Strathmore
paper
22 7/8" x 14 5/8"

39   *Cat ("25 Cats Named Sam…")*,
c. 1954
Hand-colored offset print
9 1/8" x 6"

41   *"So Meow,"* c. 1960
Ink and Dr. Martin's Aniline
Dye on paper
9 1/2" x 12 1/2"